Praise for
Whistling to Trick the Wind

In *Whistling to Trick the Wind*, Bart Edelman asks us to look at the world differently. In the opening poem, "The Woodpecker," the speaker confides, "I ask myself what I've done / To earn admission into heaven." The poems that follow explore the challenges life brings with honesty and wry humor. In "Maude Tells Claude," Edelman invites the reader to "Slowly place one foot / In front of the other." That act of slow reflection is at the center of "Truth or Consequence" as we ponder "How possible is it / To heal the heart." Ultimately, it is our heart that has grown as we take the time to read and wonder about and revel in Edelman's poems.
    –Jill Gerard, Editor, *Chautauqua*

Bart Edelman's *Whistling to Trick the Wind* captures the dilemma of humanity's timeless struggle—the desire to be free in a world full of constraints, sometimes external, but also habitually internal. The collection effortlessly weaves together the types of experiences we are sure to recognize in our own domain, and perhaps have even felt ourselves. Edelman has managed to create a world that is both unique and yet precisely our own, where, as the speaker of "Revolution" proclaims, "the only name you know / For uncertainty is fate." In "Forest? Trees?" readers will sympathize with Uncle Harry, a man of ideas, who meets with an unfortunate accident, while it is Cousin Grace, a nitpicker at heart with a "series of hideous husbands," who lives to be 99. As our journey with the poet continues, we must ask ourselves, like the speaker in "Collapsing City," whether we really are just "men and women / Gripped tightly in nature's fist, / Unable to claim reason / As anything more than chance—" or if the answer perhaps lies somewhere else, as our "future is cast / In never-ending chapters / Of truth or consequence." This is a masterfully crafted collection from beginning to end.
    –David Garyan, Assistant Editor, *Interlitq*

Whistling to Trick the Wind is at once plain-spoken and clever, irreverent and wise. With humor and exacting language, Bart Edelman tackles memory, aging, and mortality; the quotidian world of home life, work, and politics; and finally, love and loss.
>   —**Suzanne Roberts,** *Bad Tourist: Misadventures in Love and Travel*

Bart Edelman's poems are searching and direct testaments from a poet who understands the sadness of the everyday, and savors its small victories. *Whistling to Trick the Wind* is a book full of close observation and wry humor, but also of gratitude and tenderness, exemplified by the strange tale of bowtie salesman Solomon Schwartz in "Towards Sleep," and by "Go Gentle Into that Good Night," a tribute to Dylan Thomas's famous villanelle, which Edelman turns into a poem about acceptance, and a moving farewell.
>   —**Charles Harper Webb,** *Sidebend World*

"Yes, let's raise a toast to the weary," welcome each other to this era's new Theater of the Absurd, filled with home-spun alienation, "nothing but hocus pocus," existential angst, and a beautiful deadpan delivery of the past, "One crime at a time." Who better to "stir the pot," to come knocking down the door of confusion, than poet Bart Edelman? Not the "proverbial rat," the "metonymist [who] killed time with a spoon," and certainly not you or your "faithful monkey." In his latest book, *Whistling to Trick the Wind*, Edelman has "nothing to confess but sorrow" and everything to confess regarding our future's brew and thaw of joy. This wonderful book reads like a contemporary film script, an adult bildungsroman, fragile "as a pennywhistle thistle / Caught in a terrible wind" and yet robust and blessed as that overhead "blanket of stars" that just might save us from ourselves.
>   —**Elena Karina Byrne,** *If This Makes You Nervous*

Whistling
to Trick the Wind

Whistling to Trick the Wind

Bart Edelman

Emporia, Kansas, USA

Meadowlark Press, LLC
meadowlark-books.com
meadowlarkpoetrypress.com
P.O. Box 333, Emporia, KS 66801

Whistling to Trick the Wind
Copyright © Bart Edelman, 2021

Cover Art: Deborah McMillion Nering
Cover Design: James Bucanek

Interior Design: Linzi Garcia, Meadowlark Press

Author Photo: Greg Parks

All rights reserved. This book or any portion thereof may not be reproduced or used in any manner whatsoever without the express written permission of the author, except for the use of brief quotations in a book review.

POETRY / American / General
POETRY / Subjects & Themes / General
POETRY / Subjects & Themes / Death, Grief, Loss

ISBN: 978-1-956578-01-0
Library of Congress Control Number: 2021946309

for Aspen, Lillie, and Luca

Also by Bart Edelman

Poetry

The Geographer's Wife
The Last Mojito
The Gentle Man
The Alphabet of Love
Under Damaris' Dress
Crossing the Hackensack

Poems

Yellow

The Woodpecker 3
Typing Drill 4
Level 5
To Claim the Dead 6
You, You, You! 8
Slalom 9
The Chosen Few 10
All the Pretty Young Girls 12
Posture Lesson 13
Anyone but Barrymore 14
The Wasp 15
Easy Street 17
I Love You Truly, George Clooney 18
Footnote 20

Red

The Age of Belief 23
Crime Poem 24
King of the Dropouts 26
Thin Air 27
Wrestling the Bear 28
The Business of Love 30
Top Dogs 31
Maude Tells Claude 32
Anatomy of Change 33
101 Lies 34
My Candidacy 35
Currency 37
I'm Fine 38

Black

Disappearing Act 41
Revolution 43
Forest? Trees? 44
Omar's Car 46
A Bundle of Feathers 48
Collapsing City 49
The Penitent 50
Have You Ever Been to Wichita? 51
Lost at Sea 53
Chemistry Experiment (Revisited) 54
The Other Woman 57
Truth or Consequence 58
War 59

White

Revelation 63
Our Number 65
What I Wish I'd Done 66
The Shadows' Forgiveness 67
Towards Sleep 68
Coastal Lagoon 71
The New Ralph 72
Only for You 74
Never Better 75
The Promising Spring 77
Kingdom of Swing 78
Go Gentle Into That Good Night 79
How I Came to You 80
Whistling to Trick the Wind 81

About the Author 83
Acknowledgments 84

Yellow

The Woodpecker

To know the length of my shadow
Grows smaller and smaller each year,
Makes me pause in mid-thought—
Unable to complete the sentence
It seems I need serve.
I realize no escape is possible.
Fate has a way of convincing,
Even the most ardent skeptic,
We can only go so far
Before the last chip is cashed,
And we're no longer playing
With the benefit of house money.

Each night, as sleep approaches—
If I'm lucky enough to find it—
I ask myself what I've done
To earn admission into heaven.
That I often come up empty
Gives me ample cause for sorrow.
And I think the time appears short;
I must learn to do better,
Should I expect a reprieve.
When the morning mercifully arrives,
I hear my friend, the woodpecker,
Drilling patiently, outside the window.
Is his work any different than mine?

Typing Drill

Now is the time for all good men
To come to the aid of the party.
What drivel, what rot, what rubbish!
How does such nonsense originate?
Why should this be the exact time?
Who are these supposedly good men?
When should the aid spring into action?
And where is the party we are addressing?
It's all nothing but hocus pocus,
As far as I can possibly surmise,
To take focus away from the situation—
A mess of enormous confusion, indeed.

The quick brown fox
Jumps over the lazy dog,
And, at least, does so—
For all the right reasons.
No need to beat around
Anything resembling a bush,
Although I'm sure the lazy dog
Could employ one at a moment's notice,
If he might simply rise from sleep.
Regarding the quick brown fox,
What is there to say?
The sly creature likes to leap;
Let him have his day.

Level

I thought of life without levels—
All the terrain, flat and plain—
As far as the eye can see . . .
A horizontal world of duplication
Where no one bothers to enter,
And not a soul departs.
The populace eats and drinks
From the public trough—
Content for what the straight and narrow
Have to offer the status quo,
Whose rage expired ages ago.

There are bankers and brewers galore—
A few gangsters and stewards—
Each one more tired than the next.
They sleep across a vast lowland,
Arid beyond reason's measure,
Hopeless by its very nature
Or the total lack, therein.
Ah, for the equality of the even—
As odd as it seems.
Yes, let's raise a toast to the weary.
Long may they lead recumbent lives.

To Claim the Dead

He knew all along
It would have to end;
She could only be driven so far.
He didn't have enough gas
In his tank for the likes of her—
Forget the water, oil, and anti-freeze.
She had already slowly begun
To apply the brakes,
Despite her pretty feet
Resting nowhere near the pedal.

He'd been foolish to think otherwise—
Believe a future existed
When they had not embraced the past,
And the present was less than promising.
He realized she wanted to go places,
Travel in circles that made him dizzy,
Shift twice and ask questions later,
Even if she stalled out along the way.
A smart man would have seen this coming,
Stayed far out of her lane,
Allowed her to pass, with caution;
But he wasn't that man—
Far from it.

What on earth would he tell his pals
After it all came crashing down?
They'd warned him from the start,
Said she was out of his league,
And he had her picture to prove it.
He knew it was pathetic—
That he couldn't possibly stop—
Pull over to the side of the road,
Turn his emergency blinkers on,
Wait for the sound the ambulance made
When it came to claim the dead.

You, You, You!

Congratulations are in order.
You have finally arrived.
You have your own blog.
Your audience can follow you daily.
You can post what you observe.
You can post what you desire.
You can post what you think.
You can post what you feel.
You can post what you eat.
You can post what you do.
You can post . . . you, you, you!

You live inside the loop.
You keep your ear to the street.
You worship the avant-garde.
You champion the underdog.
You deplore the status quo.
You applaud the common good.
You welcome the little man.
You drive the correct automobile.
Who better to break the news?
Who better to stir the pot?
Who better to right the wrongs?
Yes, yes, yes . . . you, you, you!

Slalom

Simon thought and thought and thought;
If Trish could only learn to slalom,
It would all be good between them—
Not one bit of trouble ahead.
But she resisted his advances
And kept her skis straight forward,
Never intending to turn them
In any other direction, whatsoever.
Still, he hoped he had a chance.
Perhaps, tomorrow, she would be kind enough
To keep her knees locked together
When she began the zigzag turns—
He prayed she could master—
And glide through the set of yellow flags
On the north side of the mountain.
He realized how long it had taken him
To shift his weight to his rear foot
In order to better control his skis.
Maybe, it would simply demand more hours
For her to master a skill
He knew was inherently difficult.
Just cut her some slack,
He repeated, again and again,
Listening to the sound her breath made
In the soft bed they shared,
While he watched winter retreat,
Under a blanket of stars.

The Chosen Few

It doesn't seem to matter
How many you shepherd through;
By semester's end, without fail,
There are always the chosen few,
Those misbegotten, struggling students
Who are, unfortunately, destined
Not to make the grade.
They don't particularly flunk;
That would be too easy, of course.
Rather they tend to languish—
These fish on a hook—
Caught in a gruesome grip
From which they cannot escape:
No matter how many make-ups are granted,
How many deadlines extended,
How many absences excused.
Perhaps, it's not even their fault.
Life appears to have thrown them
The knuckle curve of the century,
And they are just going to whiff—
One way or the other—
Regardless of the number of different bats
You select for them to hit the pitch.

Other professors prefer to complain
About the anguish of grading exams,
The endless essays to correct,
The department meetings they abhor.
But that pales in comparison
To the final decree,
The ultimate measure taken,
The last excruciating pronouncement
When you stand before your student—
After a sleepless night—
And utter the fateful words,
You didn't make it, Kid.
You need a bit more practice.
Maybe next time it'll work out,
And you'll get the hang of it.
Remember, there's always next semester.

All the Pretty Young Girls

Struggle gamely with their beauty,
Fragile as pennywhistle thistles
Caught in a terrible wind,
Howling through their lives.
And what of the trouble ahead,
Disillusioned spirits seeking refuge,
Blinking out the truthful lies
No one cares to believe.
What shall become of dumb love
They hold in cold hearts,
Never to open again.
All the pretty young girls,
Choked by fate they check
At cloakrooms in restaurants—
Where they pass on dessert
And feast on sorrow.

Posture Lesson

It is expected, by now—
After months of intense practice—
We should be able to stand
As straight as a post:
No bend, no droop, no hunch,
No attempt, whatsoever,
To hoodwink the general public
Into believing we are something
Or someone, in this case,
We most certainly are not.
If we cannot throw our shoulders back
And remain uprightly erect—
In times that dictate it—
Then we simply will fail
To carry out the most basic tenet
By which this life is sustained.

How truly sad, then,
Are the crooked among us,
Stooping at the slightest provocation,
Diminishing what little self-worth
Remains to be claimed.
Yes . . . woe, woe, woe, are the weak
Whose knees forever buckle,
When they think their sunken chests
Do not know the difference
Between what's in and what's out.
And pity the poor fools,
Pretending to be in a position
They never properly assume.

Anyone but Barrymore

On his best day
He's anyone but Barrymore:
Unshaven, unkempt, untamed.
He hopes to meet a woman
Much like himself—
Who will not worry
About outside appearances,
A recent list of credits,
Money in the bank,
The proper Westside address.
He thinks, lately, he's been
On a particularly bad roll;
Fate has cooked the dice,
And they're not serving him well—
These long days and nights.

Perhaps, he needs to attend
The kinds of Bohemian places
Where his true creative calling
Comes more into focus,
Clean up his rough image,
Let the boyish charm
Take control of his life—
Even though he doesn't want
To sell his soul to Hollywood
And the first matrimonial agent
He meets on the granite street,
Filled with one star after another.
Still, a tall, elegant woman—
Slightly resembling Bacall—
Wouldn't be bad, at all.

The Wasp

It was only Thursday,
And he was already
Drinking himself into Sunday;
Mary didn't know what to do.
True, he had lost his job,
His mother had suddenly taken
A turn for the worse,
And he suffered from chronic rhinitis.
Yet the totality of it all
Finally began to make sense;
She could no longer deny it.

Thank goodness, he was asleep,
His breath labored from Canadian whiskey.
How hard could it be
To gather her belongings
Before dawn arrived and leave?
It was only a month
Since they'd been living together.
Her family was right all along,
But she had failed to listen.
What a fool she turned out to be!

And what was there between them?
Why had she selected him?
How had she sold herself short?
When did she give in to hopelessness?
It was just so very tiresome
In these cold, cramped quarters.
She thought she would die
If she spent another night there.
Nothing tied her to him;
Would he even know she was gone?

And then fatigue caught up with her.
She dreamed she was a wasp,
Yet had to make the best of her lot.
At least, she could take flight—
There was certainly merit to that.
When she awoke, hours later,
He was frying eggs,
Asking if she wanted breakfast.
Mary took a moment to think,
Flapped her wings together,
Set off for the table.

Easy Street

We were over the top—
Smart guys who knew enough to stand
At the front of the line
And never back away from trouble.

We ran with the big dogs,
Outbarking anyone who threatened
To turn us in for a reward—
Often unclaimed and unpaid.

We learned who we could trust—
In a city full of fools—
Working the nightshift numbers,
While the weak fell fast asleep.

We fixed the entire market
Before a soul realized it was broken,
Staying six steps ahead of the law,
Who followed a mile behind.

We got out of the game
When the time was right,
Left it all on Easy Street—
Lived for another day.

I Love You Truly, George Clooney

Oh, George Clooney,
What I wouldn't do for you:
Clean you, clothe you, cook for you;
Carry your protest signs
Up and down Fifth Avenue,
Challenge every single rumor
Concerning your so-called sexuality,
As if ambiguity were a crime.

Oh, George Clooney,
If you could only come home to me
Each night in Staten Island,
We'd make beautiful music
Until the wee hours, you'd see.
I'd buy you chocolates
And an array of flowers
To christen the life we'd share.
I'd swear my devotion to you
On a stack of leather Bibles,
Stretched as high as the Empire State Building.

Oh, George Clooney,
I'll proudly play Catwoman,
If you'll remain Batman.
And you won't desire Lake Como
Once you view the little nest
I've built for us on Richmond Avenue,
One story above Al's Deli,
Where the brisket and rye
Make you tremble and sigh.

Oh, George Clooney,
You won't need to save
Another soul in the world—
Once you surrender to me.
They'll be enough peace between us
You won't have to travel the globe,
Seeking another righteous cause.
O (Sweet) *Brother, Where Art Thou?*
I love you truly, George Clooney.

Footnote

It's how you view yourself now—
Nothing but a reference
At the bottom of the page—
One note employed to elucidate
A specific point well taken,
Yet, perhaps, never explained enough
To keep the reader on the mark.
In your youth you imagined
You might be more than a mere comment,
Cited on an as-needed basis—
Required evidence of the lowest order.
However, it's safe to say,
Space still remains for you,
Albeit, often, south of the border—
The last tortilla on the truck,
Bound for a single destination.
And when the text of your life
Demands examination from a source
Whose credit seems beyond reproach,
Think of all you have given
To the field of scholarly discourse,
And choose the high road—
Before you slip into obscurity.

Red

The Age of Belief

They say, on the morning news,
It's the age of belief,
But, quite frankly,
I appear faithless these days,
Checking out of my life
Every chance I get.

Perhaps, it's nothing at all,
A mere case of malaise—
Or what my friend, Fabrice,
Refers to as ennui—
This boredom of the soul
I am unable to escape.

And, yet, how convenient it would be
If I could only believe
In anything, whatsoever.
I don't need to entertain
A grand concept of God,
Or even love, for that matter;
These ideas burden the mind.

What I seek is nothing more
Than the evening breeze at my back—
Whisper of wind so free,
It never disrupts the universe.

Crime Poem

Julia was in the kitchen,
Mixing up the metaphors
She planned to serve for dinner.
It took a good deal of time,
But she went about her work,
Like elk on silk:
Ready, waiting, garnished.

It never occurred to her
To throw caution in with the turnips.
She just praised Almighty God
For the bounty she prepared,
Adding the proper ingredients
To the traffic arteries she bled
Into a slow cooker on the stove.

Her husband sat in the living room—
Arms akimbo as an owl—
Waiting for his boss to arrive,
Adjusting the height of the bar
So he could limbo his way
To a spagnanimous promotion,
After a few stiff cigars
And a drink full of Cubans.

Yet as luck would play no part
In this rather curious evening,
The boss smelled the proverbial rat
And hatched an idea of his own.
Entering the couple's residence,
He produced a red revolver,
Shooting the husband on the spot
That could never be removed.

In the end, Julia struggled
To make sense of it all.
With the husband dead as a nailed door,
And the boss arrested for carpet abuse,
She and the Schenectady Police Chief
Feasted on a diet of figures of speech,
Reciting prayers for the deceased,
While a metonymist killed time with a spoon.

King of the Dropouts

Disengage, disengage, disengage . . .
It's all I do these days—
Post retirement, if you will.
I'm the king of the dropouts,
Releasing everything I once grasped
In the heyday, hubbub, Heisenberg,
When I couldn't race fast enough
To catch the next train to Clarksville—
No matter who was at the station,
Offering me the meteoric ride.

Now, it's always summer
In the winter of my mind.
I travel where I desire,
Free to do as I please,
Measure the morning wind—
Basic directions I chart—
With nothing more than a hat
And a pair of leather boots
To keep me upright and steady—
Even on the heels of detachment.

I no longer require a home—
Just a post office box, in case
Rare news must reach me.
As far as friends are concerned,
The fewer, the better—
At least, in this realm.
It took a lifetime and a half
For me to relinquish the past,
Lock expectations in memory drawers—
Combinations long forgotten.

Thin Air

Anna sensed his uncanny ability
To grow taller and taller,
While she appeared smaller,
Shrinking by the minute—
The sweep of a second hand
Ready to do her in,
Ticking its way across her tiny face.

True, she was hardly surprised
By this wrinkle in time.
Daily she checked the mirror,
Noticing how her size
Diminished with every hour.
When he returned from work,
Each evening at eight,
She had to crane her neck so high—
Merely to glimpse him—
She often thought better of it
And crawled further away.

If he missed her at all,
He never let it be known
But kept on, splendidly,
As if they saw eye to eye.
He carried on conversations with her,
Yet she failed to understand
Anything he said;
How could she,
With his head above the clouds.
Eventually, she lost sight of him—
Unaware he was even there—
And disappeared into thin air.

Wrestling the Bear

The notion of wrestling the bear
Appealed to Sawyer when he read an ad
On the front page of the local newspaper.
As he and the wife were strapped for cash,
Two-hundred dollars was quite a payday
For someone who was out of work and dead broke;
He gave it more and more serious thought.
Upon finding the bear was housed
In a trailer, halfway across town,
He decided to pay a visit.

The bear seemed nice enough.
Sawyer could see her through a tiny window.
She was watching television and eating snacks.
That she was wearing a pink sweater—
With her name neatly written on it—
Made Sawyer feel even closer to Clare.
Perhaps, this wasn't a bad idea, after all, he thought.
Still, a deal is, certainly, a deal,
And he planned to show her no mercy.

Sawyer took an entire month to study
The proper technique for wrestling a bear.
He often visited the public library
And consulted the few folks who knew
The ins and outs of such matters.
He decided to employ the famous Swarm Offense
To catch poor Clare off guard, unprepared.
The week before the epic match
His wife sewed him a gold singlet;
Across the front it read *Sawyer the Destroyer*.

There was no formal ring for the event,
Simply a clearing near an abandoned mill.
Clare emerged with her entourage in tow.
She appeared to be the picture of perfect health,
Signing autographs for her adoring fans.
Then the mayor and town council were introduced
And a church choir sang the National Anthem, off-key.
The referee was a man named Easy Ed O'Shaughnessy,
Who Sawyer despised immediately on sight.

As soon as the contest began,
Sawyer realized he was in a world of trouble;
He had underestimated his opponent.
The first time Clare laid a paw on him,
He was unable to grab hold of her
Because she had greased herself with Crisco.
He was lucky she took pity on him—
The minute or two the match lasted—
Easily wrapping Sawyer up like a burrito,
Sitting on him, raising both furry arms in victory.

Sadly, Sawyer did not earn the money he sought;
He was inconsolable for weeks.
The mere thought of his stinging defeat
Brought on bouts of nausea and depression.
He would not leave his apartment
And wondered how he could make ends meet.
Then, as luck might immediately have it,
He heard of a touring kangaroo named Boo—
Eager to take on all challengers for a hefty prize.
Sawyer quickly shook off his grappling blues,
Exchanging them for a pair of boxing shoes.

The Business of Love

I should have retired
From the business of love
While I still had the chance,
But I was foolish
And far too unwise
For my own good.

I should have called it a day—
Refused the transaction—
Placed a sign upon my door,
Left the little shop
I opened before the war,
When hope remained an option.

I should have been clever—
Concealed my many motives—
Kept a few coins in my vest,
Never let anyone else know
The fear I fought each night,
Just thinking of being alone.

I should have realized
What it was I had to lose—
How solitude is only an offer
Until the final bill comes due—
Calculated all I'd need to pay
For my investment in you.

Top Dogs

You can always tell them
By their distinctive bark.
They know exactly who they are
And make no bones about it.
Just watch the way they stride—
The casual sway of their hips—
Frames so far leaner
Than a crisp rasher of bacon.
They're the alpha males—
Canines whose mere presence
Commands the respect and envy
Of every single hound in town.
Now and then, you spot them,
But only at the events that matter,
Where the elite meet to eat
And sample a sumptuous table—
A banquet of treats too decadent
To share with the public.
Their pedigree is unquestionable,
The proper breeding, lineage and such.
Even the framed, official papers—
On wood paneled library walls—
Attest to how much they belong
To the select, privileged few,
Who run ahead of the pack,
Sniffing a more rarefied air
Than the rest of us.

Maude Tells Claude

Maude tells Claude it's over;
She no longer has any use for him.
Their union is a sham
She won't stand for anymore.
He can take whatever he pleases;
It's of little consequence to her.
She needs to conquer the world
Without him lollygagging around,
Complaining about this, that,
And everything under the sun.
He's turned into a *flojo*—
A lazy shadow of a man,
Living off her welfare,
Spending his entire time
Entranced by the television
And the sound of his own voice.

Maude will move to Minneapolis—
Or, possibly, Cincinnati.
Perhaps, enroll in college,
Make something of herself,
So she won't be a woman
Who never advances a step past
The man refusing to remove
An axe from her back.
Still, she must face Claude again,
Before she makes her escape,
Climb through the window
She's left slightly ajar—
Slowly place one foot
In front of the other.

Anatomy of Change

We could wake up one morning
And sense an anatomy of change:
Select the largest mirror available,
Stare into it for as long as possible,
Shudder, if need be, and face the world.

We could give it a rest, at first,
Allow all opportunities to pass
Without uttering a single word,
Shrug our shoulders and smile;
Let silence be our guide.

We could make a solemn promise
To remain uncharacteristically impartial;
Think thrice and, even then, hesitate
Before we begin to speak . . .
Approach this, also, rather deliberately.

We could defer the final sentence,
Normally offered on these occasions:
Be lenient enough to propose clemency,
Have mercy on the court of appeal—
Tell the jury to take the day off.

101 Lies

You told me 101 lies—
All of them true.
You had me walk the line
Across the shadow of death,
Merely to keep me alive.
Oh, I always knew it was you;
Every hour of each day,
Teaching me how to tie my shoes,
Without the proper laces needed
To keep me upright and mobile—
Above this doubt-filled fire,
Burning the skin off my feet.

And I stood and listened
For as long as I could.
Took my soul to the cobbler,
Authorizing any essential repair
He felt was in order,
But, honestly, it did no good.
Hobbled, incapacitated, crippled;
Call it what you will.
It's all the same to the man
Whose mercy is an elaborate sham—
A hoax of such utter enormity,
I know not where it begins,
Or where it ends.

My Candidacy

I've decided to announce my candidacy
For the Presidency of the United States.
It's something I've privately pondered
But was afraid to address publicly.
However, the latest, twisted current events
Lead me to firmly believe
I am exactly what this country needs—
The antidote for an ailing nation.

First, my domestic priorities are in order.
I know, for certain, what end is up
And what beginning should never have begun.
Quite frankly, I possess a knack,
When it comes to things like that.
You might say I was born with a gift
I intend to use to my advantage.

Second, I spent a few weeks abroad in 1972,
After I misread my flight manifesto,
Witnessing the natives, eye to eye.
My foreign policy will, undoubtedly, reflect
An international understanding of diplomacy—
Touting military peace through war—
Arsenals any general would adore.

Third, I've chosen my Vice-President.
He is, literally, an attack dog;
A German Shepherd of outstanding pedigree,
Who can bark up one hell of a storm
Should the need ever arise,
And my opponent requires a good bite—
If, for nothing more, than spite.

Well, that ought to do it.
I'll be ready to protect and serve
At a moment's notice—
Give or take a month or two.
I have a very large hat
I intend to toss into the ring;
It's a charcoal beauty,
Barely covering my head.

Currency

Wanda knew the answer
Without having to ask the question.
It was not rocket science;
It was not brain surgery,
Although she realized she ought
To have her head examined
For staying this long with him.
Heads, I lose . . . tails, I lose . . .
She muttered daily,
Flipping a quarter in the air,
Catching it between her teeth,
Sampling the metallic taste,
Thinking how she'd been warned—
Time and time again—
There was nothing dirtier
Than a piece of soiled currency,
Changing hands too often to count.
Wanda rolled the tarnished coin
Round and round in her mouth,
Slipping it under her tongue.
She kept telling herself
To make a decision,
Follow through with the plan
She avoided for years.
Then she heard his heavy footsteps
Climbing up the wooden staircase.
Oh well, oh well, she repeated,
Sliding the cold coin
To the back of her throat,
Before she quickly swallowed it.

I'm Fine

My brother tells me I'm pretty.
My sister tells me I'm plain.
My husband tells me I'm fine.

My mother tells me I'm thin.
My mirror tells me I'm fat.
My husband tells me I'm fine.

My friends tell me I'm smart.
My boss tells me I'm stupid.
My husband tells me I'm fine.

My doctor tells me I'm healthy.
My monthly tells me I'm sick.
My husband tells me I'm fine.

My beautician tells me I'm open.
My shrink tells me I'm closed.
My husband tells me I'm fine.

My Lexus tells me I'm rich.
My bankbook tells me I'm poor.
My husband tells me I'm fine.

My pastor tells me I'm saved.
My God tells me I'm damned.
My husband tells me I'm fine.

Black

Disappearing Act

Let's cut to the chase:
A gun, a canary, a cocktail, and a whip.
Add a magician,
(Too headstrong for his own good)
Who answers to Otto,
But prefers to be called Fritz
When he vacates the stage.

Now, suspend your suspenders
And forget to imagine
Anything resembling a clue.
In fact, the aforementioned whip
Serves as a non-existent prop, if you will,
Nothing more than a shill,
Set to send you and a goose
Off to parts unknown—
Just for the sake of amusement.

However, there really is a gun,
And it's quite fully loaded
With equal measure of whimsy and charm—
Enough to disarm even the most skeptical reader,
Objecting to this sanguine act.
As far as the canary is concerned,
She sings, out of tune,
So that the audience pities her,
Yet appreciates her effort, nonetheless.

Regarding the cocktail's inclusion?
Why, the success of the performance
Demands an inscrutable devotion to detail—
And the various ingredients the magician dispenses—
Throughout the stirring time
He's allotted above the footlights,
Before he turns the stage dark.
Then, he and his faithful monkey
(Surely, you knew there was a monkey!)
Disappear into smoke so thick,
We simply call it night.

Revolution

You think there must be
A right for every wrong,
A man for every woman,
A nest for every sparrow.
It never occurs to you
To question if the earth
Still spins on its axis,
The moon has lost its glow,
The flood arrives too soon.
You go about your business,
Leaving nothing to chance,
Because it does not exist
In the world where you live—
And the only name you know
For uncertainty is fate.
You follow your faith each day,
Filled with the good sense
To understand how kindness
Presses the universe ahead—
One revolution at a time.
You, who are without fear,
Do not abandon hope
In those of us who remain
Unsure of our next step,
Unsteady on our feet,
Uneasy along the path.

Forest? Trees?

Who cares if it's impossible
To see the forest for the trees.
What are a few minor details, anyway.
Big picture, little picture . . .
It's pretty much all the same
When you get down to it.
If you stare long enough
At an object in question,
God knows what you'll perceive.
And is it really for better
Or worse, in the long run?

Take my dear Uncle Harry;
He was particularly keen on realizing
The entire scope of a project—
How it seemed to work together
On a grand scale.
He was an ideas man,
Taking synergy to another level,
Always squawking about amalgamation
And the world view from space.
Yet, one fine autumn day,
He walked directly into traffic
And came face to face
With a Lexington Avenue bus.
That, my friend, was that—
So much for the weight of it all.

And then there was Cousin Grace,
Who never met a concrete fact
She failed to embrace,
Clinging to it for comfort's sake—
In her tiny studio apartment on 8th Avenue,
Where she nitpicked her way through life
And a series of hideous husbands.
She lived to be 99!
Yes, who's to say what's right.
Forest? Trees? Trees? Forest?
It's pretty much a crapshoot, at best,
Or, at least, as far as the eye can see.

Omar's Car

Omar arrives promptly at 5:35 a.m.
To take you to Burbank Airport.
He's driving a spanking new Toyota Prius,
And he's courteous beyond measure.
You can tell just how proud
He is of this automobile—
How swell it's appointed and maintained,
The care it's received.
He offers you mints, gum, water—
Anything to make your journey
A bit more pleasant,
Providing a choice of music channels
And the proper ventilation for comfort.

Omar proceeds down the Golden State Freeway,
Driving reasonably and cautiously,
Unlike the other Uber drivers,
Hell-bent on speeding and weaving
Along their desired routes.
He confides in you . . .
Lets you know about his primary job,
Working the 3 to 10 p.m. shift
At a local fast food restaurant in town,
His two daughters and three sons,
And a wife who tells him to slow down,
Or he'll suffer a heart attack
Before he turns 50.

Omar reveals he loves the Uber gig,
Meeting a variety of nice folks
And scheduling his own hours.
Life is, indeed, good to him,
God is great and kind,
And Omar is full of the Holy Spirit,
Pointing to the St. Christopher medallion,
Prominently displayed on the dashboard.

When you reach your destination,
You exit Omar's shiny vehicle,
And he extends his hand to you.
You take it in yours,
Amazed at its sheer enormity
And the gentleness his grasp commands.
You pivot to approach the terminal,
Glancing back one final time
To nod and thank him for his service,
But he has already disappeared.
You know you will never meet him again—
Although he will revisit you often.

A Bundle of Feathers

One bird is much more
Than a bundle of feathers,
My grandfather would always say,
Winking and nodding at me,
As if I knew what that meant.
I didn't—and still don't,
But I think I'm getting closer
To his revelation each day.
And he looked like a bird,
Especially in his later years,
Measuring himself against the sky.
He often spoke in a sharp chirp,
While his head shook back and forth,
Contemplating his ultimate fate
From the top of a tall tree.
I could see how his mind worked
And his heart loved to sing,
Despite the Parkinson's disease,
Ravaging his thin, bony frame.
When it was time to leave us—
Weeks after his bride of sixty years
Departed this good, green earth—
He found a secluded place in the barn,
Removed the clothing he wore,
And prepared for his long sleep.

Collapsing City

It happened so quickly
Who knew what to think?
One moment it was there
And the next—gone!
How was it possible
An entire city could collapse
In a manner of moments?
Everything, more or less,
Destroyed to such an extent—
The ground was all that stood
In the wake of the ruin.
And we who first stumbled
Onto the empty street,
Held our breath and wept
While we surveyed the scene;
What else could we do?
An investigation began
For clues to uncover
What caused this disaster,
But the search proved futile.
In due time we realized
We were just men and women
Gripped tightly in nature's fist,
Unable to claim reason
As anything more than chance—
Small town inhabitants
Without a place to call home.

The Penitent

The penitent sought atonement
For his most egregious sin
And stood in the rabbi's study,
His feet unsure of the floor.
He promised himself to end
The mendacity and deception—
Hallmarks of a miserable life,
Leaving him worthless in the light,
Wifeless in the dark.

He knew what the rabbi would offer—
A certain sense of consolation
And prayers for a soul
He felt was near dead,
Stamped with an expiration date
He was unable to read—
No matter what bifocals he wore.
Perhaps, he thought, it was all a show,
And the poor rabbi deserved far better
Than to listen to a man
Whose only truth was his latest lie.

By the time he abandoned the synagogue,
The penitent realized he would never return
Until the consequence of his transgression
Embraced the offense he could not escape.
To be welcomed into the house of God
Required mercy and forgiveness
He had yet to discover.
And, above all, there was still love—
Devotion so utterly overwhelming,
He had nothing to confess but sorrow.

Have You Ever Been to Wichita?

When she asked me,
Have you ever been to Wichita?
I thought I was dead.
I might as well have carried
The dreaded doornail in my pocket—
Or a fish upon my head—
The stinkier, the better.
At least, that might have prevented me
From being so forthcoming,
Ordering a third drink,
Giving her a second glance,
Before realizing she was my first wife.

Listen, the lighting in the bar
Had to be God-awful, to say the least.
And she was, undeniably, wearing
One of her numerous wigs.
Still, I should have picked up
Any of a hundred clues:
The voice with the Brooklyn lilt,
The laugh like a jackhammer,
The eyebrows, always in mid twitch,
And the fingers, of course—
Nine digits in motion,
Counting everything in sight.

She'd told me, when I met her,
Amnesia ran in her family—
History so cruel, it could easily outrace dawn.
And, now, I firmly believed,
The malady had caught up with her.
Yet, she kept curiously watching me—
Until the time I excused myself—
Insisting I reminded her of someone familiar.
When I reached the street,
I heard her softly call after me:
Perhaps, it wasn't Wichita, at all.
Have you ever been to Des Moines?

Lost at Sea

You waited too long this time
And knew what that meant.
Now there was no safe return,
No sanctuary in sight,
No harbor for light—
Retreat, utterly hopeless.
You heard before of men
Who wandered too far from shore
And became lost at sea,
Simply because they failed to accept
What nature offered them,
Fishing for the kind of humility
Their pride could never allow.
Yes, foolish is the pitiful love
A sailor makes to the mistress
From whom no escape remains—
Only the eternal rest he takes,
Slipping gently beneath the waves
To embrace the green grave.

Chemistry Experiment (Revisited)

Dear Ms. Macklin,

Thank you for your email;
I'm glad you enjoyed reading my poem
In your college anthology text
For your Introduction to Literature class
At the University of North Alabama.
You ask what I was thinking
When I wrote "Chemistry Experiment."
You also want to know
What themes are present in the work,
And if the poem merely refers
To a lab experiment gone awry
In an academic setting of sorts,
Or if there is something more there—
Perhaps, an incendiary relationship
That explodes in the faces of those
Who conduct this trial in the laboratory?
Finally, you need whatever info I can provide
By 11 a.m. tomorrow morning,
Because you've chosen the poem
To complete an oral presentation for your class,
And you are determined to succeed,
Quite possibly, *snag an 'A'*
From your rather demanding professor.
Ms. Macklin, I certainly understand the predicament
That has you, *at your wit's end.*
It is a knotty problem, indeed.
So let's see what we can achieve together.
Tonight, I seem to have a generous spirit,
And sleep won't arrive for an hour.

We'll give it a whirl then, my friend,
And see what we uncover.
First, concerning the matter of theme:
Your guess is as good as mine.
I didn't have one in mind
At the time I wrote the poem,
But, yes, okay, there are quite a few
Lurking around the old lab
And one or two on a black table
Underneath the tall Pyrex beakers.
Lift them up carefully and sneak a peek.
You're plucky enough to come up with one;
Just think universally, of course!
As for the *tricky* main characters,
And whether there could possibly be
A bit more to their *academic* relationship
Than meets the naked eye,
Yes, you're right, no question there.
Who mixes assorted hormones
(Oops! substitute chemicals)
In an open, liberal, flammable environment
And doesn't expect an explosion or two
To rock their way through the semester.
Surely, Ms. Macklin, you know of such events?
And, if not, accept my humble apologies
For being too presumptuous, at this late hour.
So, good luck in your endeavor.
I'll be keenly interested to know
How you make out on your assignment.

Do remember, please, to steer clear
Of the periodic table and all that rot.
I wish I could simply say,
Sometimes an element is just an element—
But, too often, I'm afraid, it's not.

All the best,

B.E.

The Other Woman

The other woman—
Always someone's wife—
Tells amusing tales
When her husband exits the room.
A cocktail in hand,
She pitches back and forth—
Story after story revealed—
A pure sense of disdain
At the mere mention his name brings
When she utters it in vain.
And they are, surely,
A rather curious couple,
As far as unions go:
He, the rough and tumble lawyer;
She, the type of woman
Society breeds for such a man
Who displays his wife,
Like a reticent poker hand
He seems ready to play,
But only when the chips are down.
And they survive the endless parties
To which they're invited,
Entertaining the highbrow crowd
With their cat and mouse game—
Until the ripe night of endless rain
Demands she load the Luger
He keeps by the bed,
Before discharging a bullet
Straight through his head.

Truth or Consequence

We'd like to think—
If we knew then,
What we know now—
We'd rewrite the book
We call our history,
Erase the tasteless errors
Spilling across each page,
And recreate a past
To reflect the present,
Whose future is cast
In never-ending chapters
Of truth or consequence.

Why must it be
This need of ours,
To right every wrong
We could not foresee
On the crooked road,
Always gripping our destiny.
How possible is it
To heal the heart,
Reveal a novel story
From start to finish,
Unburden the guilty mind—
One crime at a time.

War

There was a war in session,
But we never thought, for a moment,
We were fighting on the front line.

There was a war in progress,
But we were led to believe
The casualties were few and far between.

There was a war in motion,
But we had been stopped, suddenly,
Unaware that fate came too late.

There was a war in denial,
But we kept to the script,
Even if the words were unintelligible.

There was a war in silence,
But we heard each exploding shell—
And the death knell it rang.

There was a war in absentia,
But we had already fled,
Needing this world no longer.

White

Revelation

When my father revealed
He once murdered a man in Canada
At the age of 19,
It failed to surprise me.
He never told me the exact details—
And I never asked—
Knowing the admission was more than enough.
He was 92 and ready to call it a life.

The few times I saw him,
Before the end finally came,
He referred to it as *the incident,*
And he seemed to feel, perhaps,
My total lack of reaction
Gave him permission to mention it, again,
As if this were his dying request.

The last day I visited him,
I gathered up the courage to question
Whether my mother knew
About the so-called *incident,*
At any time before she passed away,
But he simply muttered, *Never,*
Paused for a moment,
And then said, matter-of-factly,
I'd rather kill myself,
Than admit such a thing to her.

After my father's death—
For the first time since I was a small boy—
I began to wish I were not an only child,
Remembering how lonely I felt
On certain weekday afternoons—
In the white heat of summer—
When the weight of tomorrow
Had not yet arrived at my front door.

Our Number

I've got it right here—
Tucked inside my left pocket—
Saving it, just in case
We need the combination
To open what might be closed
If things go south between us
Some dreary, misbegotten night,
And we find we've grown apart . . .
Hating ourselves for it.

I've got it right here—
Hidden within my shoe—
A correct set of digits,
The perfect code for survival,
Should it come to this,
And it's our last hope—
One final attempt to rescue us both
From the tomb of the dead,
Where grace makes a space
For the place between us.

I've got it right here—
Pressed against my chest—
An inch above the heart
I've carved for you;
No need to add, subtract, divide,
Multiply, quantify, or identify
What remains of the figure
We agreed to long ago,
When all we knew was love.

What I Wish I'd Done

Graduated high school,
French-kissed my second cousin,
Allowed my beard to grow out,
Hang glided when I had the chance,
Sung in a heavy metal band,
Quit that job in the circus,
Married the dancer from Detroit,
Tried to make amends with my parents,
Cried at my best friend's funeral,
Kept my given name,
Opened a hipster bar,
Escaped the *Me Generation,*
Purchased a larger house,
Waxed the dog each weekend,
Lent my jigsaw to a neighbor,
Neglected the yard work more often,
Yelled less at the postmistress,
Bought that little blue Miata,
Uncorked better bottles of wine,
Vowed to learn the tango,
Drawn at least one self-portrait,
Run the Boston Marathon,
Judged nobody but myself,
Zipped my mouth shut each morning,
Invoked the *Serenity Prayer* at night,
X-rayed that tumor much sooner.

The Shadows' Forgiveness

I spend a lifetime,
Learning the shadows' forgiveness—
These apparitions of doubt—
Whose extra frequent visits
Make me face the face
I wear on a daily basis.

I rise each morning
To conduct the week's business—
Breakfast in my belly,
Ledger by my side,
Totaling what I eat
And what I spend—
A balancing act to set me straight.

But when afternoon arrives,
The first illusion appears—
Often in a suit of mismatched threads,
Offering to propose a new contract
And exchange our prior terms
For something more profitable—
On his end and mine.

The evening vision who enters
Between the portals of one dream
And the signpost of another,
Never plans an extended visit—
Only long enough to sprinkle
What remains of destiny's dust—
A reminder how reprieve lives . . .
Despite the absence of light.

Towards Sleep

Solomon Schwartz seldom slept.

In fact, if the hard truth be known, Solly hadn't slept for years. Honest. His lack of sleep boggled the minds of doctors he sought for treatment. And there wasn't a sleep clinic in any of the five boroughs that wasn't familiar with him.

Lately, Solly had taken up quarters in the spare bedroom of the apartment he shared with Gert, his wife of forty years. Since their marriage, they had lived in the apartment on Bleeker Street in Greenwich Village. Now that Solly was almost wholly without sleep, he decided it would be cruel to keep Gert up each night with his own restlessness, so, long before midnight, he left Gert and quietly made his way across the hall, where he buried himself in books and television to help pass the unforgiving nights.

Solly was a freak of nature—plain and simple. The last time he had actually slept for more than a moment was the summer of 1979. This meant he had a four decade hiatus from the nocturnal dreams of you or me. To say he was perpetually tired, even downright irritable, would be understating the understatement—and then some.

No one knew why Solly had dispensed with sleep, including the so-called medical professionals. Yes, they pricked and prodded him, no end. They ran tests and walked him through a series of examinations and supposed treatments but, utterly, to no avail. And he, himself, was completely flummoxed, always at a loss for words to explain his predicament. It just seemed to happen. Much like the *D* train pulling into the subway station on time. Or a delivery man from Domino's ringing the doorbell and presenting you with a pizza you don't believe you ordered, especially if it has anchovies. Yes, sir. Simple as that—really. Often, life has no meaning, whatsoever.

But back to Solly and his plight . . . The poor man racked his brain, day and night. He tried to conceive a secret he must be keeping from Gert or any of the three children who called him Dad. Had he entered into an adulterous affair? Swindled his partners in the bowtie business, out on Long Island? Dishonored his cherished parents before they passed away? Good G-d! Lord Almighty! What would keep a man of his ilk from finding consolation on this earth? It was such a basic question, he thought. Yet, night after night, week after week, month after month, and year after year, poor, poor Solly hadn't as much as a clue.

And, in the meantime, Solomon Schwartz became somewhat of a celebrity. The New York newspapers, hungry for the famous, or infamous, devoted columns to him. Magazines spewed articles concerning his condition, and the doctors, of course, filled journal after journal with medical jargon and various explanations for *the man of wonder,* aka *the sleepless bowtie salesman of the night.*

As if this weren't enough for Solly, there were the endless psychiatrists, who shrunk him, left and right, up and down, and, on occasion, sideways. Even his children were confused and refused to visit him, often cowering in a corner when they felt guilty enough to show up on a major holiday or two.

Eventually, Gert couldn't take the pressure. One Sunday morning, out of the blue, it appeared, she ran off with a jeweler from Queens. Solly was mortified and embarrassed, to say the least. The children sided with their mother and dispensed with him entirely. For the first time in his life, Solomon Schwartz turned to drink. At first, it was merely beer, then a bit of white wine, then red, then highballs, then martinis, and, finally, he graduated to bourbon. It was a descent of unsettling proportions. And despite the booze and a dash of depression, as well, Solly still could not sleep, self-medicated or not. Indeed, there was no solace for Solomon Schwartz.

A few months into Solly's dizzyingly deep alcoholic spiral, he agreed to one last appointment to see a sleep specialist who came highly recommended—from the neighborhood bartender, no less. The doctor wanted to run a few medical tests on Solly before delivering his diagnosis and sent Solly to, yet, another hospital for extensive examination. After the battery of tests were completed, Solly was on his way out of the hospital when he became disoriented and ended up on the wrong floor, entering a random room. There he saw a woman patient who transfixed him, immediately. The fact that she was comatose, meant absolutely nothing to Solly.

Soon, with the permission of the woman's family, and the support of his various doctors, Solly began spending extended periods of time with the woman who never knew Solomon Schwartz existed. What she did, though, was put a smile on his face for the first time in years. Solly's drinking dilemma magically disappeared. Solly became a changed man—a devoted partner whose life was enriched beyond measure. In this good woman, Solly found his refuge.

And when it came to pass, it was only silence that eased Solomon Schwartz towards sleep.

Coastal Lagoon

I am unsure of lust,
Residing in curious places
Where I would never suspect:
The eye of a tree,
The belly of a rock,
The toe of a cloud.

I do not presume to know
How to find desire
Around the jolly corner,
Over the next bluff,
Under the back steps.

I become somewhat flustered—
All too often, I'm afraid—
When I pretend passion
Thinks on its feet,
Sings for its supper,
Dreams of its demise.

But I have, most recently,
Witnessed the afterglow
Love casts across the floor
On a candlelit night,
In a circular room,
Beside a coastal lagoon.

The New Ralph

It's what I am:
The new Ralph—
Pure and simple,
Easy and clean;
This name I've earned
To move about the world,
Conduct the business of life.

I'll answer when called—
Respond to the title
I've approved for myself,
After all these years
I've attempted to be
What it is I'm not.
Now I can travel freely,
Meet the folks who matter,
Without the swindles and lies
I've employed for disguise.

What a complete transformation.
The advent of truth liberates
The common man in us all.
I shall never return
To a race not worth winning—
Spinning out of control,
A hundred revolutions per minute.

These days I've stepped away from myself,
Inherited a curious wind,
Once arriving two weeks too late.
Hey, I'm the real deal—
Evander Holyfield in a can—
A member of my own clan.
I take my place at the table,
Order whatever I please,
Seize the moment to proclaim:
I am the new Ralph.

Only For You

You, my boom baby boom,
My room with a view,
My brew on a winter's night.

You, my Katzenjammer kid,
My bid for the grand prize,
My eyes, ears, nose, and toes.

You, my go-to gal,
My pal of a million moons,
My dune across the sand.

You, my tender muse,
My cruise down the Nile,
My smile, a mile wide.

You, my woman, my mate,
My fate through the ages,
My pages . . . only for you.

Never Better

We are sorry to hear you are deceased.
The registered letter quickly got my attention,
Unsigned with no return address.
As far as I knew, I was alive—
Or as much as at any time
In the near or recent past.
I do have a penchant for long naps,
But not the eternal kind.

Certainly, this was puzzling.
Had my demise made headlines?
I checked the local obituaries,
Contacted each hospital in the vicinity,
Surveyed my neighbors down the block,
And, eventually, questioned my wife.
She had more than enough reasons
For wishing I might have met my Maker.
However, no one knew a word about my passing.

Slowly, though, I began to believe the news.
I often found myself glaring at the mirror,
Checking my pulse once an hour,
Barking at the dog for reassurance.
Finally, my wife could take it no longer
And put me outside for the night.
I was in a state of utter confusion.

Then, one day, I went to the market—
For the first time in months—
To purchase a pack of menthol smokes.
When I offered the cashier money,
He just laughed hysterically and said,

The dead pay no bills in this establishment.
Who, in his right mind, would want their cash?
By God, his words were electric.

Suddenly, I was at peace in the world.
I carried my letter everywhere I went
And paid for nothing at all—
Not even a stick of gum.
Even my wife agreed to leave the house with me,
Although she always kept a leash in her purse.
Now, I enjoy being dead;
Never felt better in my life!
Just wish I had departed years ago.

The Promising Spring

He was beginning to accept
The promising spring—
An offering she would bring
When she arrived next week
With the groceries and the mail
She constantly kept for him
Through the long winter months
In this part of the frozen tundra.

That he needed to be alone,
Endure the harshest climate imaginable,
Embrace his total isolation,
Seemed foreign to her, at first,
But she was a patient woman
Whose devotion rose far above
A notion dismissed as love.

She knew not what brought him
To his own sense of reckoning,
And never thought to ask,
Realizing there was a private religion
For every state of contemplation.
Now, a worn path measured
What distance remained between them.

Yes, soon, the thaw would be evident,
The welcome sight of birds overhead,
Time for another season's arrival—
A renewal to witness hope.
And they would bake the bread,
And they would shake the bed,
And they would wake the dead.

Kingdom of Swing

I came to find my place,
A calling you might even say,
Perhaps, a little late in life—
My feet light, but my burden heavy.
Once I heard the music though,
I was never quite the same.
Yes, Ma'am, I knew I needed to dance,
Morning, noon, and well past midnight.
If there was so much as an hour
Without my signature moves,
I was, frankly, beside myself,
And two of me, dear sweet Lord,
Became one too many to handle.

I went clubbing, clear across Harlem,
Long before there was a name for it.
I carried Benny, Cab, and Louie,
Deep down in my back pocket,
And let Duke and The Count
Ride right up front near me.
I did the Lindy without the hop,
And the Jitter between the bug.
I could Charleston you into tomorrow—
Merely given half the chance.
These days, I'm a bit slower,
Far closer to heaven than hell.
But I look forward to that big dance
I'll be performing right on cue—
At home in the kingdom of swing.

Go Gentle Into That Good Night
(After Dylan Thomas)

Please, please, go gentle into that good night,
Old age should never burn at close of day;
And do not rage against the dying light.

Wise women at their end know death is right,
Because their words leave little left to say;
Please, please, go gentle into that good night.

Good women watch each wave and see how bright
Their deeds have danced across a silver bay,
And do not rage against the dying light.

Wild women catch and sing the sun in flight,
They learn to let grief hurry on its way,
Please, please, go gentle into that good night.

Brave women, near the last, adjust their sight
Through eyes that search to find a final ray,
They do not rage against the dying light.

And you, my mother, climb the lofty height,
Bless every step you calmly take, I pray.
Please, please, go gentle into that good night.
And do not rage against the dying light.

How I Came to You

Bankrupt . . . petty . . . poor . . .
Without a drop of honey
Coursing through my veins—
The ire from another life
I led in slow motion—
When my soul departed
The moment I turned away
To scowl at the stars.

Aimless . . . shiftless . . . stuck . . .
In nothing except the mire
I could not escape,
But grew to embrace,
Because once you wear
The cloak of loneliness—
Day in and day out—
You don't know how else to dress.

Admit . . . permit . . . submit . . .
Vows I refused to keep
Until I came to you
And heard you reveal them
For the first time—
This gift, a blessing,
To free me from myself.

Whistling to Trick the Wind

Ran out of words—
One letter at a time—
Found no use for them.
Spoke in speechless sounds
Only the deaf can hear.

Lost his job,
Refused to repeat destinations
The train passed as it wound its way
From the mouth of Manhattan
Through the belly of Brooklyn.

Gave his friends the heave-ho
When they requested an intervention,
Paid the neighbors for their services,
Climbed up the roof in the dark
And communed with the moon.

Came to believe in a God
Whose perfection was never in question,
Promised to wire his mouth shut
If the Almighty would agree
To keep his miracles to himself.

Lived a rather fruitful life
In the company of boulders—
Too old and tired to converse—
Took his final act of contrition,
Whistling to trick the wind.

About the Author

Bart Edelman was born in Paterson, New Jersey, and spent his childhood in Teaneck. He earned both his undergraduate and graduate degrees from Hofstra University. He has taught at Kingsborough Community College of the City University of New York, Santa Monica College, West Los Angeles College, Long Beach City College, UCLA, and Glendale College, where he edited *Eclipse*, a literary journal. Most recently, he was appointed to the Affiliate Faculty in the MFA Program at Antioch University, Los Angeles. Edelman served as Poet-in-Residence at Monroe College of the State University of New York. His work has been widely anthologized in textbooks published by City Lights Books, Etruscan Press, Fountainhead Press, Harcourt Brace, Longman, McGraw-Hill, Pearson, Prentice Hall, Simon & Schuster, Thomson, the University of Iowa Press, Wadsworth, and others. He has been awarded grants and fellowships from the United States Department of Education, the University of Southern California, and the LBJ School of Public Affairs at the University of Texas at Austin to conduct literary research in India, Egypt, Nigeria and Poland. In addition, he received National Endowment for the Humanities grants for a series of lectures at public libraries on "The Common Good: Individualism and Commitment in American Life," and "Trails: Toward a New Western History." Collections of his work include *Crossing the Hackensack*, *Under Damaris' Dress*, *The Alphabet of Love*, *The Gentle Man*, *The Last Mojito*, and *The Geographer's Wife*. He lives in Pasadena, California.

Acknowledgments

Some of the poems in this collection first appeared in the following anthologies, journals, and other publications:

"Go Gentle into That Good Night" in *Bryant Literary Review*

"The Age of Belief," "All the Pretty Young Girls," "Maude Tells Claude," "Truth or Consequence," and "The Woodpecker" in *Chaparral*

"Coastal Lagoon," and "Lost at Sea" in *Chautauqua*

"The Business of Love" in *Flint Hills Review*

"Anyone but Barrymore," "Footnote," "How I Came to You," and "Whistling to Trick the Wind," in *Interlitq*

"To Claim the Dead," in *Coming Off the Line: The Car in American Culture, An Anthology*, in *Main Street Rag*

"Thin Air," in *The Sand Hill Review*

Gratitude, well beyond measure, to Susan Cisco, Charles Harper Webb, Linzi Garcia, Kevin Rabas, Tracy Million Simmons, the staff at Meadowlark Press, and Kim, who contributed their time, devotion, and good cheer to *Whistling to Trick the Wind*.

Meadowlark POETRY

Books are a way to explore, connect, and discover. Poetry incites us to observe and think in new ways, bridging our understanding of the world with our artistic need to interact with, shape, and share it with others.

Publishing poetry is our way of saying—

>*We love these words,*
>*we want to preserve them,*
>*we want to play a role in sharing them*
>*with the world.*

www.ingramcontent.com/pod-product-compliance
Lightning Source LLC
Chambersburg PA
CBHW021429070526
44577CB00001B/132